Harry Harefield
FROM THE WOUNDS OF LOVE

Poems of love won and lost

Harry Harefield
FROM THE WOULD S OF LOVE

Poems of love won and lost

MEMOIRS
Cirencester

Published by Memoirs

MEMOIRS
PUBLISHING

1A The Wool Market, Dyer Street, Cirencester, Gloucestershire, GL7 2PR
info@memoirsbooks.co.uk   www.memoirspublishing.com

From the wounds of love

All Rights Reserved. Copyright © 2013 Harry Harefield

No part of this book may be reproduced or transmitted in any form or by any means,
graphic, electronic, or mechanical, including photocopying, recording, taping
or by any information storage or retrieval system, without the permission
in writing from the copyright holder.

The right of Harry Harefield to be identified as the author of this work has
been asserted in accordance with the Copyright, Designs and Patents
Act 1988 sections 77 and 78.

The views expressed in this work are solely those of the author and do not
necessarily reflect the views of the publisher, and the publisher hereby
disclaims any responsibility for them.

ISBN: 978-1-86151-133-1

FOREWORD

I have always been a thinker, a deep thinker.

Anyone who is a deep thinker knows that it goes hand in hand with a deep desire to be secretive about one's feelings, especially feelings of the heart.

With me, when a thought enters my mind, I work it through so many scenarios, trying to think it through to a natural conclusion. Sometimes I am not able to move on, returning to that thought again and again.

During the time I spent fishing on Harefield Lake number 3 (in Uxbridge, to the west of London), I had so much time to torture myself with. One day I thought, why don't I write it down? I started forming verses in my mind. This came naturally to me, so I took out a little pocket diary I had with me and started writing.

When I had finished that first poem, 'My unfulfilled love', I felt a great sense of release. Finally I had got the thought off my chest, and I could move on. Yet when it came to putting my name to such emotive feelings, that was a step too far, too soon. So I decided to write 'Words by Harefield Lake 111'. Then I had a second thought and decided to make it sound like a normal name. I settled for Harry Harefield, and everything else that followed carried that name.

So Harry Harefield is a PLACE.

I had made two previous attempts at writing poems before. The time I can clearly remember writing a poem was around the time of a broken heart, so it is no coincidence that my heart inspires me now to pick up a pen and get it off my chest so my brain can rest.

So it is with more than a hint of trepidation that I have decided to publish, and bare the contents of my soul to the world. The strangest thing to me on reading my poems about love again is how every time it always feels like the first time. This seem to be my Achilles heel, but the genie is out of the bottle now, and what will be will be.

James J.

WORDS ONE

A love story

HISTORY IS A BROKEN DREAM
(CHAPTER 22)

I wonder if you think of me
after you told yourself I'm not the one?
I wonder if you need my words
to make you sparkle, blush and glow?

I'm stronger now, and it's in the past
It was an eerie world of lost romance
I can still remember feeling lost
and the trust I gave you, to my cost.

It was a learning time of a different world
where hopes and dreams seemed a fairy tale
then harsh reality came along
and reminded me why I had been strong.

Past frustrations ebbed away
as I focused on your broken trust
I vowed then that I would not return
to that place of dreams where I got burned.

As I turn to face fresh adversities,
the strength I've gained from renewed faith
and the peace I've found within myself
will come outside and spread around.

I'm weary now from battles fought
some won, some lost, inside my head
but the hand of fate still holds the key
to the land of peace and tranquillity.

CHAPTER 1

MY UNFULFILLED LOVE

Out of the blue
I said I loved you,
You said you cared too
but you've been there before
and the wounds are still deep
because of the love you still keep
for the one that you've waited for.

I said I would wait,
till the day we're both free
to quench the desires
of my unfulfilled love.

Little did I know
when I left you that day
that my heart was breaking in two.
The hurt went on long
and I needed to be strong
to stop myself falling apart.

The worse has now passed
says my poor aching heart
well if it will keep
why do I weep
for my unfulfilled love?

CHAPTER 2
WHEN LOVE COMES CALLING

My heart's been broken once or twice
I thought I learnt my lessons well
I'd treat my partner oh! so nice
that when love came calling I would not fall.

There I was, I'd seen it all
I'd known some girls, I'd had a ball
I thought there was no way
that I would stray
then your love came calling.

When love comes calling
big or small, weak or strong,
there's no defence
you can only hold out for so long.

You asked about my other half,
I'm afraid to face a grief that size
she thinks we're having troubled times
I've kept it so well hidden,
she hasn't even realised
that for me, love's come calling.

Where will it end? only time will tell
when did I first look in your eyes?
when did the spark first ignite?
it doesn't matter now, the wheel has turned
because love's come calling.

CHAPTER 3

I CAN BE YOUR ONE AND ONLY

When I first looked in your eyes
I told myself it could not be true
but somehow it feels all too real
so all I can do is to follow through.

When I first looked in your eyes,
I was confident, you seemed so shy
now I see you looking oh! so cool
is that to make me want you more?
or is that to play me for a fool?

With every mention of your 'friend'
it's like a dagger turning in my heart
but I don't think he means that much to you
so I'll just keep on following through.

The look in your eyes says you care
I know from your past, you've been hurt before
that's why I'd never leave you lonely
I can be your one and only.

I might have to face that day
when I'd realize that you don't want me
I'll be strong and I wouldn't wait in vain
until that day, I'll keep following through.

CHAPTER 4

WHAT TO TELL THE CHILDREN

What can we tell the children?
how can we explain
that the love that drives us together
does not mean they should be in pain?

A child needs its mum and dad
to show them order in their lives
how can we explain the complications
and assure them there's no competition?

To live my life could be so simple
but without your love it would feel so empty
can the children understand
the growing pain within this man?

Loving you I might regret
but what will leave the greater pain?
to not have tried, or to have failed
or to fulfill this love I feel inside?

CHAPTER 5

THE PAIN OF DESPAIR

This morning I awoke with the strangest feeling
I was feeling very down
it seemed to me my dream had ended
it was over before it had begun.

Since the day when I first courted you,
I've been like a drowning man
wishing you would throw a lifeline
to stop me drowning in a sea of love.

All I needed was to hold you
and tell each other 'we'll be all right'
but all you showed me was your kindness
you kept your love locked up inside.

Now I fear the dream is over
and I'm in need of peace of mind
I can't go back to as it was
because love for her I cannot find.

Yesterday the wheel was set in motion
I need to find where I belong
can I deal with all the pressures
that breaking up will bring along?.

CHAPTER 6

WHY I LOVE YOU SO
(THE DREAM GOES ON)

Just to stand there
and to watch you in your loveliness
and to talk to you,
and gaze into your eyes,
explains to me why I love you so
and yet to try and say....
There are no words
that can explain.

I can see no way through
those barriers that stand between us
and yet, to fuse our souls as one
as I lie asleep in your arms
that is the dream, and it goes on.

I believe in love
and I believe in luck
and I believe in fate
and I believe in faith
and I believe in me
and I believe in you
and I believe my dreams
will one day come true.

CHARTER 7
THE SACRIFICE

How can I just walk away
from someone that I love so much?
help me to show the patience
that must surely bring its just rewards
the quest? to give you your time and space
to learn my love is all you need.

I've hurt so much for so long
to win your love, that's all I ask
I've turned each way, looking for solutions
and still ahead remains a task.

Time will tell whether my quest for love
will flounder on the rocks of guilt
or whether dreams do come true,
and with you I'll walk into the blue.

CHAPTER 8
THE FLAME OF PASSION

I still have the burning desire
to hold you close and make love to you.
I still feel the need to say
how much I love you, and want you so.

I believe you're now ready to love again
after all the years of hurt and pain
all that remains for me to do
is to beat a clear path to your door.

I believe I now have the strength
to hold myself back and wait for you
the only thing I need to believe
is that a flame still burns in your heart for me.

We can never be sure of love's first choice
but isn't that part of life's mysteries?
to take a chance with your heart on fire
hoping fate will guide us to our heart's desire?

CHAPTER 9

A VALENTINE (FEBRUARY 14TH)

I've never known a love so intense
the want for you remains immense
everything I see or do
makes me want to be with you.

I lie awake at night and think of you
with every woken moment comes a thought of you.
There's a well of tears beneath the surface near
that will not fall, despite my fears,
It's been near so long but will not flow
are they tears of joy
or tears of sorrow?
I'll find out soon, maybe tomorrow.

CHAPTER 10
THE FINAL CHAPTER?

I brought it on myself
I forced your hand.
I cornered you, so you spoke your mind.
I once said we're both alike
and I did to her, as you did to me,
I'm sure we felt the same relief.

You delivered yours with some style
you looked beautiful, I wished you were mine
you passed your 'note' without a word
it was quick, it was clean, it left no stone unturned.

When I read your words my stomach sank
my legs went weak, how faint my heart felt
it was the most savage 'put down'
I've ever been dealt.
I just wanted to crawl and hide away.

This seemed to go for an eternity
I could not even retreat with dignity
you see, I had been playing for keeps
for the highest stakes
I was willing to do whatever it takes.

having placed all my eggs in one basket
and now seen them smashed
what could I do?
now my dreams are trashed.

I wished I had not made that faithful call
but I was scared to death
I know now why
instinctively, I know when something's wrong
I could not stop myself
the impulse was too strong.

Recovery came with surprising speed
I thought, when in a hole, your digging heed.
I just thought, stop, do nothing
and let time heal.
It hurts you put the blame on my head
she brought it on herself,
now the feeling is dead.

I know that there is no way back
it does not mean I'll stop loving you
it just means I'll now leave you alone
and wish I had not been wrong all along.

CHAPTER 11

WHEN I PASS YOU ON THE STREET

What is it about you
that has me feeling this way?
why can't I pass you on the street
and just see another woman, on her way?
With just one fleeting glimpse of you
and I feel like I felt on that first day.

I thought I had overcome the loss
of the battle I fought for your love
but now I'm hurting once again
because I saw you once today.

I got the message that you sent
that you were his, and my dreams were spent
it was strange as I watched the two of you
I had been through this scenario once before
it puzzled me, I could not think when
but I remembered my feelings felt the same.

I remembered then it was in a dream
it was a different place
but everything else the same.
I knew then that I could cope
with the parting of the ways.

I'm stronger now than I've been for a while
I'm looking forward now
and trying not to look back - that was
until I passed you on the street.

I focus on the cruel things you've said or done
to give me the will to move on
the will is strong and my mind is clear
I'm starting to think, I was almost there
until I saw you on the street.

CHAPTER 12
I'M NOT MADE OF STONE

Does it make you happy
to see me this way?
Does it please you to know
that I just can't let go?
tell me what to do
to bring to an end
this pain in my heart
because I'm not made of stone.

Am I the man of your dreams?
I just need to know
or has my love been in vain?
why do I need to suffer the pain?
I've tried to work out
what I mean to you
but everything's a contradiction
are my perceptions fact
or are they just fiction?

I'm dreading to hear
the words you might say
I mean nothing to you
it was just a passing phase
but I have to face up
to the hard facts of life

that my love has been wasted
and it's time to move on.
I can't go on like this
because I'm not made of stone.

CHAPTER 13

I DON'T WANT TO BE ALONE

When I remember those long lonely nights
and the cold empty days
when nothing seemed right
and the thoughts of despair
that accompanied the gloom
it reminds me again
I don't want to be alone.

When I look at the love
I have in my heart
and I think of the dreams
that have since departed
and I'm wondering where
I can go now from here
I only know, I don't want to be alone.

I must find a place
where I can be at ease with myself
where my heart is contented
and I'm at peace with my love
you'll remain in my heart
and I'll be keeping the faith
that one day you'll be mine
and it will all be worthwhile
because with you by my side
I'll never be alone.

CHAPTER 14

WHISPERING SILENCE

I thought I had it all
and I wanted for nothing
except a thrill in my heart
and the excitement of loving
you came into my life
like a whispering silence
all of a sudden it's you
that I've lived my life for.

Why should it happen to me
at this stage in my life?
I'm married with children,
a home and a wife
although I don't love her
there seems no way out
and now I feel lonely
because I'm not in your life.

I'm looking for answers
deep in my thoughts
sometimes I feel happy
when I'm sure you love me
then it comes back to facing
the hard facts of life
I'll forever be lonely
because I can't make you my wife.

CHAPTER 15

WHAT IF?

What if, I never kiss your tender lips
or feel the softness of your skin
or smell the warm scent of your hair?
And what if, I never see the beauty of your breast
or taste the nectar of your love?
and what if, I never sit and listen
to the wonder of your voice
saying 'I love you too'?

And what if, I never have to heed
the calmness of your reason
and sense the comfort of your touch?
then I have never lived
and I will go to my grave
with eternal regret.
What if, you were to be my wife
and you were to have my child
and our souls would be as one
and what if you were to be with me
and you did love me too?
my life would be complete
and my dreams would have come true
and I'd always stay with you.

CHAPTER 16
I'LL SIT AND WAIT

I did not know I was looking for love
I thought I was guided
 by a star from above
I've always felt lucky
in the life I have led
I've been through some crises
and came through them well
feeling much stronger
and with confidence to face
the challenges of life, and whatever laid ahead.
Now that I've met you
and I know I'm in love
knowing I can't have you
is driving me nuts
but there's nothing I can do
so I'll just sit and wait.

CHAPTER 17

THE LOVE OF MY LIFE

Sometimes I think
it can't be real
it's not happening to me
these things just aren't true
well if it's not real
why do I hurt
and think only of you?

This can't be real life
things don't happen this way
me, a grown man
like a schoolboy in love
it seems like I'm putty
in the palm of your hand
although I see reason
it's not healing the pain.

When I look back
at this time in my life
will I shamefully hide?
 pretend it did not happen
and did not hurt my pride?
I'm sure I'll be truthful
and admit to myself
I missed a chance of a lifetime
with the love of my life.

CHAPTER 18

WHAT HAS LOVE DONE FOR ME?

It's sapped my strength
and drained my will
I've lost confidence, and self-belief
It's broken my heart
and bended my knees
that's what love has done for me.

It could have been different
it still could be good
if you could show that you love me
I'd be waiting for you
I don't know where I'm going
I don't know what to do
it seems you've got me guessing
is it over for good?
It feels like I've never loved someone
like this in my life
I've tried to remember when
but it's just out of sight.
It seems I hardly know you
but you're there in my thoughts
I try to deal with the fact
you're finally gone
but each time I see you
I want to break down
that's what love has done for me.

CHAPTER 19

SAY THAT YOU LOVE ME

I've waited so long
for the moment you'd call
to say that you've missed me
and want to see me again
but with each passing day
you're further away
from my arms where you ought to be.

If I can't be with you
just say that you love me
We'll take one step at a time
but I just need to hold you
to feel you, to love you and...

So just say that you love me
and it's with me that you want to be with
I've waited so long
and my love is still strong
and my will to succeed still firm.

so just say that you love me
and set the ball rolling
see where destiny takes us
to the place where we want to be.

CHAPTER 20

YOU LOOKED AT ME THAT WAY AGAIN

It seems such a long time
since you left me behind
and out of your life for good
I had started to think
that I must have been wrong
and you must have been right all along
because I had told you my thoughts
I could leave well alone
quite satisfied, my love for you
you could not doubt.

I still can't understand
why you're acting this way
why you continue to make me feel small
because I've done nothing wrong
I've left you alone,
no telephone calls. Harassment? no way.

I was taken by surprise
when I looked in your eyes
and just for a moment we stared.
I was forgetting myself,
when you remembered your cool
and calmly, you just looked away.

I was embarrassed at first
I thought, you've done it again
you've gone and rattled my chain
I asked myself why,
I thought of the look in your eyes
then I knew why
you looked at me that way again
I wish I knew what was in your heart
when you look at me that way again.

CHAPTER 21

THE HAUNTED
(A MONKEY ON MY BACK)

I'm still haunted by dreams of you
can't you hear my silent tears?
it's not something I want, or even something I need
I just can't escape these thoughts of you.

I've tried to move on, I've really wanted to leave
I've got on with my life
I've found other things to pursue
but I still can't get away
from these haunting, silent, thoughts of you.

You wounded me, you really made me bleed
therefore I must have been bad, some time in my life
because there's no way you can ever justify,
your cold and thoughtless, wicked act.

You gave me the reason not to trust you again
I know it won't happen, I'll never call you again.
so now all that is left is my words and your reasons
and the haunting, silent, thought of you.

So we await the day in your life
when you'll want me again
what will I do? I will never forgive you.
Somehow you've enchanted my heart
and I cannot escape you
so I'm stuck here in limbo
with the haunting, silent, thoughts of you.

CHAPTER 22

HISTORY IS A BROKEN DREAM

I wonder if you think of me
after you told yourself I'm not the one?
I wonder if you need my words
to make you sparkle, blush and glow?

I'm stronger now, and it's in the past
it was an eerie world of lost romance
I can still remember feeling lost
and the trust I gave you, to my cost.

It was a learning time of a different world
where hopes and dreams seemed a fairy tale
then harsh reality came along
and reminded me why I had been strong.

Past frustrations ebbed away
as I focused on your broken trust
I vowed then I would not return
to that place of dreams where I got burned.

As I turn to face fresh adversities
the strength I've gained from renewed faith
and the peace I've found within myself
will come outside and spread around.

I'm weary now from battles fought
some won, some lost, inside my head
but the hand of fate still holds the key
to the land of peace and tranquillity.

CHAPTER 23

THE SADDEST PLACE I'VE EVER BEEN

Every once in a while
I'm taken right back in time
to a place I just can't define
except to say…
it's the saddest place I've ever been.

When I don't see you I'm fine
you're just a distant memory in time
and what I'll never understand,
why your humiliation?
and why do you want to keep up these ties?
I was just a nuisance, wasn't I?

Is it your warped sense of fun?
or is it feelings you've tried to deny
that keep you preening yourself,
and showing that you're fine
in the hope that you catch my eyes?

But I try not to look
because the hurt just returns
and the bridges you've burnt
mean I'll never feel the same
yet still it remains,
the saddest place I've ever been.

You once claimed I'm a fiend
who won't leave you alone
yet not one week goes by
without you taking your time
to make sure I notice you.

I used to dream of the day
when I could take my revenge
when you would say,
you really did care
then I could spit in your eyes
and I would just walk away.

Now I don't feel that way
I only look to the day
when a thought of you, a glimpse,
or even there in my face
no longer means
the saddest place I've ever been

It's occurred to me since,
if you really are showing
that's it's my attention you're seeking
evens if it's to massage your ego
so if YOU can't let go
it really must be,
the saddest place you've ever been.

WORDS TWO

(A Divorce Story)
Chapters One + One to Eight (Epilogue)
January-July 1997

WORDS CHAPTER 1

THE HUSBAND'S TALE (FOR THE CHILDREN)

It's not the path I chose to walk
she's made her choice and I'll see it through
if she feels it's what I deserve
after all I've done for her,
then this is what she must do,

She can't touch me, I've thought it all through
I've done the best I can, there's no regrets.
I wanted to leave some years ago
I'd had enough, I wanted out
but my quest for love was all in vain
so I chose to stay and hid the pain.

Now I feel fine and don't have much fear
only my children's needs, and emotional fare
keeps me looking back to show I care
she can say what she likes,
she can tell her lies and do her worst
I've seen through her, I know her curse.

In years to come she'll remember me
as the best man she has ever known
she'll wonder why it all went wrong
she'll remember my spirit, she tried to break
but whatever she did, I still stayed strong
and bid my time, for however long.

When she looks my children in the eyes
Will she tell the truth or will she lie?
She'll try to blame me for their pain
The selfish bitch, so smug, so vain!

She won't touch me, I know she can't
whatever she does, my conscience is clear
she made her moves, had her affair
I silently watched because I knew
she set the agenda, and I'll follow it through.

WORDS CHAPTER 2
DON'T CRY MY BABIES

Don't cry my babies when you think of me
your daddy's there, with thoughts of you.
I tried my best to keep you safe
and to make you strong, and feel secure
but the hand of fate has dealt a blow
to the dreams I had to raise you pure.

The harm's been done and the hurt goes on
and there's nothing I can do to ease the pain
of separation forced on us,
so it's with patient calm I wait my turn
to talk to you and show my love.

You've thrilled my life, and made my dreams
you are my world, you make me proud.
So don't cry my babies, instead shout aloud
because your daddy's there, with thoughts of you.

WORDS CHAPTER 1 - (REVISITED)

THE HUSBAND'S TALE - (FOR THE WIFE)

It's not the path I chose to walk
You've made your choice and I'll see it through
If you feel it's what I deserve
after all I've done for you,
then this is what you must do

You can't touch me, I've thought it all through
I've done the best I can, there's no regrets.
I wanted to leave some years ago
I'd had enough, I wanted out
but my quest for love was all in vain
so I chose to stay and hid the pain.

Now I feel fine and don't have much fear
only my children's needs, and emotional fare
Keeps me looking back to show I care
You can say what you like, you can plot your schemes
You can tell your lies and do your worse
I've seen through you, I know your curse.

In years to come you'll remember me
as the best man you have ever known
You'll wonder why it all went wrong
You'll remember my spirit you tried to break
but whatever you did, I still stayed strong
and bided my time, for however long.

When you look my children in the eyes
will you tell the truth or will you lie?
You'll try to blame me for their pain
You selfish bitch, so smug, so vain!

but you won't touch me, I know you can't
Whatever you do, my conscience is clear
You made your moves, had your affair
I silently watched because I knew
You set the agenda, and I'll follow it through.

WORDS CHAPTER 3
A WIND OF CHANGE

I stand alone, as men sometimes do
A wind of change is on the way
The world I built remains detached
I've felt alone throughout the day.

To see my children standing there
They're close to me, yet far apart
I feel the need to turn away
They've been sold a line, it breaks my heart.

When I was young, I felt alone
without a father's guiding hand
now I have children of my own
I want to spare them that same loss.

It's strange to me looking back
I was the only person I could trust
As I look for comfort in myself
life's gone full circle - but I'll be back.

My heart is good, and my faith's in truth
I protect myself, and hold my own
If I can live my life the way I choose
then I'll win much more than I'll lose.

My sunny days will come again
I'll find someone, of this I'm sure
who'll need my love and make me proud
to have been true to myself throughout this drought.

WORDS CHAPTER 4
FREE FROM YOUR RAGE (A CELEBRATION)

As I survey the loss of the world that I built,
from the isolated quiet of my old lonely room
through the mist and the fog, that could have spelt doom
comes a euphoric feeling, I'm free from your rage.

It's a wonderful feeling, to know I can breathe
I can dream, I can wish, I can do as I please.
I don't have to answer to your selfish demands
from now in my life, I'm free from your rage.

The lessons you've learnt, as you lived by the sword
stokes this fire in you, that you cannot control
in spite of your rage, and the venom you spit
I sit here with comfort, I'm free from your rage.

The material things that I stand to lose
and the needs of my children, that gives me the blues
means that there is a downside, with worse still to come
at least I look forward, because I'm free from your rage.

I know you are driven, by a desire to hurt
to bend me to my knees, and then watch me squirm
but the joke is on you, as I'd seen it before
I've spent years just wishing, to be free from your rage.

You made your choices, and I'm paying the price
I'm acting with calmness, and keeping my cool
I should be crying, and regretting my loss
Instead I feel happy, I'm free from your rage.

WORDS CHAPTER 5
THE STRANGEST DAY

(The Non-trial Of Jimmy Jack)

It was a rainy day
in the month of June.
The 25th day - was that a summer's day?
As the rain came down
it felt more like
The starting of an Indian monsoon.

I was due in court
to face a charge
of ABH and assault
I was innocent
It had been engineered
the victim of a wife's falsehoods.

I had prepared my brief
with loads of facts.
Witnesses were summoned
with a threat of contempt
The prosecutor felt she could not pursue
her client's tale, now seemed subdued.

She asked my brief, would I consider
a compromise, and be bound over
she reasoned that should I accept
my clean record stayed,
and the crown justified.

I was outraged, I'd done nothing wrong
To clear my name, and the truth displayed
was my only aim,
and I would not be swayed.

For five months now,
I had been victimised,
evicted from home and vilified
for the first six weeks
my children's link
had been severed
what about their need?
They too had been crucified.

It was the most vindictive act
by a woman whom I had treated well
and with whom I had shared my life
and whose trust she had lost.

Things had started to go wrong
when she would not learn
people need their space
it's a human thing.
So to fence me in, she would socialise
and come home late
so I would apologise

But I had compromised
as far as I could.
My fishing days were very few
and there was no more that I would do.

So we went in court
and a request was made
To see the judge, to see what he could do
The briefs they went into chambers
I sat in court, with seething anger.

It was my legal right
to be tried
or to clear my name
and my cost returned
but for the expedience
of this crown court
The judge made a decision
that astounded me.

He'd read somewhere, some trial judge
had bound someone, without consent
so therefore he too had the right
to bind me over, it was his court.

But wait a minute
I had not been tried
and I had not confessed, I was confident
That they had to prove I had done wrong
It's a British right
to face down your accuser
with the jury's help
I'd be the winner, not the loser.

Now that's a poser, for the court of appeals
I've done nothing wrong
Yet I've truly been shafted
how can it be justified?
This historic judgement
on that rainy Wednesday,
This strangest day.

WORDS CHAPTER 6
AN UNUSUAL AFFINITY

I watched a fight the other night
Two warriors fighting for the crown
of baddest man in the land
and the right to be crowned world champion.

As the fight began and blows exchanged
an old familiar taste returned
Tyson knew he'd met his match
who'd bested him the fight before

What could he do, he was in a fix
He'd told the world, he was the man
for 12 years now he'd bullied his way
with the watching world, TVs transfixed.

There was no place to run, nowhere to hide
could he take his beating like a man?
Like hell he could - a foul, he cried.
and sank his teeth in his master's ear.

It was a cowardly, savage thing to do
to spit out an ear, and lick your lips
was that the defining act, from man to beast?
or a sneaky escape, from certain truth?

As I watched his act of savagery lust
he'd lost his head, there was no sense
he could never gain the world's respect
he did not care, he was in fear.

for a moment there was an affinity
with my current fight, with my ex-wife.
she'd played her game and fooled around
then could not face a taste of her own brew.

So she spat, and snarled, and screamed obscenities
to the forces of law, and planned her schemes.
Throughout it all, I stood firm
like Holyfield, a warrior, bloodied but unbowed.

WORDS CHAPTER 7

TO SARAH, MY DAUGHTER (A FATHER'S LAMENT)

I can't express this hurt inside
to think I raised you as my own
I comforted you in times of need
and cared for you when you were sick.

We spoke of the test of a character
when one is faced with a choice in life
to do what's right or what's easier
and to live with that choice
for the rest of our lives.

I prided myself as a man of truth
who stood his ground, when he was wronged
now I read where you say I bullied you
and frightened you to the point of tears.

You may not have written the faithful words
but you signed your name,
at the end of the page.
I know you know it's a load of lies,
You're my daughter, you promised you'd tell the truth
I can't believe you'd say such things.

We both have to live with the choice you've made
I hope you've learnt a lesson here
to be at peace with yourself
that's all that's required
to go forth in this world,
with your head held high.

WORDS CHAPTER 8

THE BITTER END

They say divorce leaves a bitter taste
for the emotional part, I'd been prepared.
But now it is clear what you've done to me
I find my heart is full of hate.

For 12 years now I treated you
to the best a man could hope to do
I took you off the welfare state
taught you to drive, and bought you a convertible

With every penny that I earned
and every minute I could spare
I built a home fit for a queen
and furnished it with every care

I had never strayed before you did,
and stayed at home to ease your mind
Yet that for you was not enough
so you went out searching,
to see what you could find.

Once my trust was lost, there's no going back
so we had to make the best of what was left
to raise our kids in a balanced way
with lots of love, and all we could afford.

I never gave you troubled times
I kept my counsel in my mind
although I knew I loved you not
my natural kindness still shone through

Now it seems you've forgotten all I've done
now it seems you want everything as yours
I can't even cross my door, or make a call
or see my kids, when I want to.

An average person with half a heart
would recognise what I've been through
and could accept I've done no wrong
it's just two people who'd grown apart.

But no, not you, you're not satisfied
You made Sarah sign a load of lies
now I'm not only divorcing you
but also my step-daughters too.

The hate I feel is burning bright
That's not my style, it's against the grain
but as I look to carry on
I remember your worst you said you'd do.

Well, how did it feel when I did mine?
I used my words as a surgeon's knife
to expose your lies and your game plan
Yet still you achieved what you set out to do

I hope there can be a peaceful end
but the way I feel, that's not possible
If I never speak to you again,
for the rest of my life
It would still seem like a day too soon.

WORDS (EPILOGUE)

AT PEACE AGAIN

I've found my tranquil peace again
On the lakeside where I once despaired,
As the midnight breeze made the shadow dance
it felt as if I was free at last.

It's been a long time since I felt this way
now I must look to what the future holds
To find a home and place to live
and reflect on the sunset of the recent past.

I'm glad I had the chance to do my best
to give my all, and prove my worth
although it ended in a ruthless way
I would rather this than the other way.

If I had made the moves that she has made
I know I would have betrayed my children's trust
There's no comfort of another woman's arms
that would have taken away that sense of guilt

Now the deed's been done, and I feel fine
emotionally I feel very strong
There's no need to rush into anything
I'll just take my time, and enjoy this peace.

SOLITUDE IS A NATURAL PLACE

I nearly met that girl today
the one that's the answer to all my dreams
I nearly met her enchanting gaze
and nearly asked her for a date.

Was she the one with dark, mysterious eyes?
Or the one with eyes like pools of liquid love?
Or was she that one with the wicked smile
That suggested warmth and love inside?

I'll never know till the timing's right
I always seem to miss the mark
but deep inside it's never felt
like it did three years ago.

I'm held down by this sense of hate
brought on by those unjust acts
because I know I have been wronged
I cannot rest until it's right.

I have to wait and bide my time
and come to terms with all I've lost
because what I'll gain, will mean much more
in the longer term, when it's all said and done.

I've been calm throughout this test
and try to keep all bitter thoughts at bay
I've felt alone throughout these times
it seems solitude is my natural place.

BECAUSE I KNOW YOU LOVE ME
(TO MY CHILDREN)

When my times seem so hard
When the sun just won't shine
or the birds will not sing
of glad tidings to bring.

When the stars close their eyes
and the moon goes to hide
There's a beacon inside
that's always shining so bright

It's a feeling of joy
It's a thrill in my heart
It's the comfort I need
of knowing that you love me.

WORDS THREE

Another failing in love

CHAPTER 1

A BIRTHDAY ODE (TO A FRIEND)

Well, another of your birthdate's gone by
another of our summers past
it seems to go quicker each year
we should try and make the good times last.

In another world, or another life,
we could have been more than 'just friends'.
but it could not be, our paths never crossed
except at work, in a formal way.

But we have become friends, in spite of that
and care for each other in our own way
and I would have liked to have made
your birthday wish come true
if only I had known, what I had to do.

(REPRISE PART TWO).

CHAPTER 2

THOUGHTS OF YOU

I find my senses turning to
thoughts of you, and a wish gone by
a strange feeling of expectancy
fills the air and stirs in me
exciting thoughts of a forgotten dream.

I'm trying to keep a lid on it
not wanting to raise my hopes too high
so I'm trying to get my timing right
and make sure that it's a two-way thing.

I'm drawn to you by a hidden force
self-denial has been your chosen course
I've wanted you for the longest time
maybe now in our lives, the timing's right.

I want to hold you close to me
and feel your heart beat next to mine
if fate dictates it was meant to be
then why deny the chance to try?

CHAPTER 3 (TO JULIE)

MY MESSAGE TO YOU

Is it the way that you stand
or the fall of your hair
that attracts me to you?
or is it something else
that I haven't worked out?

I can't remember when I first noticed you
and I can't remember if I've ever thought of you
but I sense we're attracted
it's been there for a while
and when we first spoke,
I felt quite uneasy
and felt I had been disturbed.

I know you've been fighting
this attraction we feel
is it an age thing?
or other circumstances not right?
I'm not sure what I'm starting,
or where it will end.
but I'm wise enough to know
that dreams are not given
but have to be made.

I may be presumptuous
to start talking this way
but you've had time to think it over
and to know what you want.
so my message to you Julie,
is to stop fighting this fate
open up your heart
and let this 'love-thing' begin.

I'm not looking for a wife
or even a permanent thing
I'll just follow this adventure
to wherever it goes.
I don't want to hurt you
and can't promise I won't
I just want to hold you
and show you I care.

CHAPTER 4
A FOND FAREWELL

It seems that I've stirred up
some emotion in you
that borders on hate,
but could yet prove to be love.

You think that I haunt you
and you can't be at ease
and I'm some kind of monster
that won't leave you alone.

That's not what I'm about
and deep in your heart, you must know it's not true,
I'm just a regular guy
with feelings I just could not hide.

I've accepted your statement
that my judgement was wrong
and it's only a matter of time,
till we leave it all behind.

I hope you've accepted
that I meant you no harm
and it was a tall order
when you've just left your childhood behind.

but it's my nature to try
and reach for the things that I want
and your love was the one thing
I wanted inside.

When you look back
at this time in your life,
and when you remember
the way that you felt
was I really a creep?
and someone you just couldn't trust?

Whatever the outcome
it must be time to call it a day
I won't bother you again
now you know how I felt.

So I'll say a fond farewell
and will always be wishing you well
it was just that these strange feelings
had to be said.

CHAPTER 5

WHY ARE WE STILL SHADOW DANCING?

If we've both let it go
then why aren't we at peace?
I've been trying to hide
the things that I'm feeling inside.

But you've said it again
that you don't want to know
not even a greeting
not goodbye, or hello.

You've spoken again
of the looks that I give
and you think that it's dirty
and it's the looks of a spiv.

Then why are we dancing?
in this non-existing affair
and why do I move you
to play with your hair?

It's driving me crazy
the things that I feel,
but I know it will pass,
because there's no wound left to heal.

It was just a man's fantasy
to meet someone new
someone he could care for
just one in a few.

well, that's the way that I see it,
how is it for you?
I believe you're a headstrong young lady
that won't hear from your heart.

Your head will find a thousand reasons
why you shouldn't be with me
but deep in your heart
there must be a doubt.

The difference between us
is that I know what I want
and you're sure you don't want me
but I'm there in your thoughts

Could it be that you're frightened
that there might be truth to the myth?
and if you ever hold me
we might never let go.

The truth is I love you
and I'm aching for you
but all that means nothing
if you're not feeling it too.

so stop this shadow dancing
and make it quite clear
it's for me that you've waited
and say that you care.

CHAPTER 6

A CHRISTMAS WISH THAT DID COME TRUE

As '97 draws to a close
a year of woe and troubled times
with grace and patience I stayed the course
and await the beginning of the new dawn.

It's Christmas time, a time for cheer
with the beaming faces of children's joy
with my heart beating a hastened beat
I make a wish for your heart to keep.

You were the one my heart's pursued
I don't know why it just chose you
could it be that it's in our destiny
or just a forlorn fantasy?

Tonight I await my fate with you
with my stomach tied in knots of fear
if it weren't meant to be, I accept my fate
knowing I did try with a loving care.

When the year began my two greatest gifts
were my children's love and my self-belief
as I look to the start of '98
the bond remains, and I can say to myself
'I believe in you'.

It wasn't all bad this passing year
because I'm now free from her poisoned rage
with still a chance of my Christmas wish come true
to make this the last one, without you.

CHAPTER 7

IN LOVE WITH YOU

I could pretend like you do
that I feel nothing for you
and my heart is not breaking in two
but I'd be living a lie
and the pain feels so real
but I still try to hide how I feel.

I have laboured so long
for the moment to come
to hold you and show how I feel.
It's been as near as it's far
from the day we first met
until now where it seems a lost dream.

There's no more I can do
I have waited for you
to tell me, you love me too
but you are so contrary
you act like you hate me
then in your eyes I can see our baby.

I should just give up the ghost
and call it a day
and look for a fresh start elsewhere
but I've fallen for you
and there's not much I can do
if I could, I would, I swear.

CHAPTER 8

WORDS FROM THE MIDDLE OF A BROKEN DREAM

It feels like I have lost again
after all I've tried to win your love
I've waited patiently for you
 to tell me you feel something too.

I want to stop and start anew
in search for the love that I once knew
but how can I start again
when in my heart, I still want you?

It's been so long since I first tried
to win your heart and show I cared
I've let all other chances pass me by
just aiming for 'Pie in the sky'.

I am a fool, to the world it seems
to love someone, before we've met
if I could turn it all around
I'm sure I would not hesitate.

But such is life, I feel so lost
I cannot find someone to trust
I have not spoken of the things you do
that keep me down, yet still wanting you.

There are times when I'm sure you feel the same
when I've I looked at you and know you care
sometimes we've spoken, as if we are one
then the door you slam right in my face.

What can I do? I do despair
I'm out of luck and out of hope
I wish I could leave it all behind
and stop thinking of you through the night.

Maybe you're not ready for a man like me
who would fill your life and serve your dreams
and love you with a heart that's true
and fulfilled all our fantasies.

I knew you were the one for me
because I saw you once upon a dream
with your mane of hair and spirit bright
and the naturalness of an earth woman.

One day soon I'll smile again
when all this pain will fade away
but for now I will just carry on
hurting in this broken dream.

CHAPTER 9

MY HEART BELONGS TO YOU

This is no ordinary love
that I'm feeling in my heart for you
it's like a big screen epic
just like the film 'Titanic'.

In such an imperfect world
where true love and trust are hard to find
when you meet someone who feels right for you
you should do all you can to hold on to.

I'll give all I am, and do all I can
to make this dream of mine come true
to be with you my whole life through
just being there and loving you.

Don't be afraid of this love I feel
because I know you know where it's coming from
you remember me from years gone by
in what was then a young girl's dream.

Time's gone by and life's gone on
yet still I'm there right in your heart
could you really live your whole life through
Never regretting I'm not holding you?

It has not yet come to a natural end
but all my cards are on the deck
it's up to you to show you care
or to close the door for evermore.

CHAPTER 10

TO JULIE

This is your truth (four years on)

The very first time that you had seen me
even before our eyes had met
I reminded you of someone,
someone you might want to meet.

They had told you all about me
it seemed I was someone no one disliked
they placed me high on a pedestal
that no normal person should deserve.

There has always been a chemistry
from the moment that we spoke
I thought I saw in you an image
of what I thought true love might be.

You came across to me as someone
with a natural beauty and so raw
a real earthly person, with a natural grace
I could see it right there in your face.

I can't explain the feelings
any better than I've tried before
and I have long come to terms
with the nature of us.

What you see in me now,
is what you saw in me then
but what I see in you now
is "let's play a game," but you are only pretending.

So face it now Julie
this is your truth
you can say that you hate me, and I mean nothing to you
but you are only kidding yourself,
I know it's not true.

JULIE ET JIM - ROMEO & JULIET 2007 (10 YEARS. ON) (AN EPILOGUE)

Now all our bridges have been burnt
Without a tender word of love, ever spoken
Or a warm embrace, or a kiss ever taken
How sad is this? It takes the p**s

Yet none of it I could have changed
Caught in a web of our 'chemistry'
I lost control of all my senses
Common sense, the first to go.

In the best of lights, it was an adventure
Of true romance, that was doomed to failure
It was our chemistry that made it happen
And it was our personalities, why we could never be.

It's like the poles of opposite magnets
When nearby, there is the strongest attraction
But when close together, if the wrong poles meet
That is the point, they can never meet.

That is the final conclusion, that I have reached
Because it ALWAYS affects me when we meet
When we are apart, there are no reasons
To waste my time, on this futile search for a one true love.

WORDS FOUR

A new beginning.

Fran – ongoing?

CHAPTER 1

THE WAY THAT I FEEL (TO FRAN)

Sometimes words are not enough
to say the things I feel inside
the joy I'm feeling in my heart right now
has been there since the day we met.

It feels to me you are the one
I've waited a whole lifetime for
everything just seem to fit
I'm living out a fantasy.

I feel you feel the same way too
because it's there whenever I look at you
to me you are so beautiful
your heart, your soul, your body too.

So let's not wait and waste our time
let's get to where we want to be
to be together all the time
today, tomorrow, and for always.

CHAPTER 2

AFTER THE WILDERNESS YEARS

I am seriously overwhelmed
by these feelings that I have for you
with a sense of déja vu
I've dreamed of love like this before.

After many years in the wilderness
where I've had to live through two false dawns
when twice I've loved someone I would never hold
under a cloud of depression, and forebode.

I thought true love was not meant for me
and Camelot had passed me by
and I would never find that holy grail
that lovers of the world search for.

But now you've come and fill my life
it still feels like a fairy tale
like I'm in a feel-good fantasy
like a kid in his/her own candy store.

I am at peace and in love with you
and everything to me feels right
I've learnt so much of what it means
so much so - I'll never let you go.

CHAPTER 3

A LOVE SO DEEP MY HEAD HURTS

I love you with such intensity
so deep it causes my head to hurt.
if I hold you in my arms too tight
I'm trying to fuse us into one.

I think about us all the time
the way we fit each other's lives
it feels like you were heaven sent
tell me you feel the same thing too.

To me you are my perfect love
you seem to fit in with my style
we don't have to be speaking all the time
to understand the things we mean.

Right now I can't wait for you
to be back at my side tonight
where I'm sure we'll spend our lifetime through
being thankful for this thing we've found.

CHAPTER 4

THE THINGS YOU DON'T REVEAL

Sometimes I feel I'm all at sea
on an emotional wave of insecurity
it stems from the things you don't reveal
your hopes, your dreams, your sincerity.

Is it enough just for you to be holding me?
not to speak about the things we need,
not to say the things I need to hear
to tell me of the things you fear?

I want to know I am the one
the rest of your life is depending on
that everything that has gone before
has led you to this open door.

You've now found someone that you can trust
who you can tell your secrets to
and shower me with all your love
because you feel I'll never betray you.

But while you keep all this inside
I'm never sure quite where I stand
am I just another stage door John
who's helping you to pass the time?

Otherwise, this is a superficial thing
if you can't say the things you feel
just in case I break your heart
and send our dreams back to the start.

CHAPTER 5
WITH ALL OF MY HEART

I'm thankful for this love I've found
here with you at this time in my life
now all that is left for us to do
is to cement this bond, with you as my wife.

I spent a lifetime searching for
this special person I can be with as one
now all I do is think of you
never wanting to be alone.

I've written of past loves I've lost
and wondered why it never was
but now that you are here with me
I learnt the lesson of the frog and prince.

You're everything I could ever want
it's been a breeze since we first met
and it's getting deeper by the day
can't you tell whenever I look at you?

I presume (haha!) you feel the same way too
it's there whenever I'm holding you
and now you know I appreciate
the love you give, and the love we make.

I dream one day we can have a child
with health and strength like the two of us
if it's not meant to be, I can still say
I will be loving you - with all of my heart.

CHAPTER 6
MY FEELINGS

I've given my best, God! how hard I have tried,
to show you, you were the one for me
but now I feel it's not good enough
for you to give your trust unconditionally.

The signs you've shown, and the things you did
showed you wanted more than I can give
I've thought it through and for the life of me
there's nothing more that I can do.

You wanted my wedding finger bare
to act as if you did not care
and when I did the same thing back,
you thought it was a vicious act.

You speak of the things I do not do
like kissing and caressing you
I must admit I let you down
there's no excuses, I should have tried.

But the worrying thing that troubles me
is the feeling that you've been using me
I've spoken of the cost of life
and your generous heart, as long as someone else is paying.

The choice you made without consulting me
shows a selfishness beyond compare
when I think it through I cannot find,
a reason to treat me this way.

Maybe you'll find what you're looking for
a millionaire to pay your way
and someone who will kiss your arse,
and pamper to your every need.

CHAPTER 7
THE PSYCHIC'S TALE

I'm watching my dream disintegrate
and there's nothing I can do or say,
I cannot shake myself awake
because this isn't about a dream of sleep.

If I had the power to change things round
tell me what you want of me
the thing that's not fulfilling you
the other things that I should do.

You say I haven't changed at all
that's the whole point, I've bared my soul
I always try the best I can
unless I feel it's not worthwhile.

My philosophy of life
is to give and take evenly,
and if one should take more than they want to give
then I reserve the right to take my leave.

I do not want this thing to end
god only knows how I've loved you
I need you more than anything
that I've needed in my life before.

This 'trust' thing you threw up in my face
it's as if you wanted me to be guilty
so if you knifed me in the back
of course it would be my mistake.

I've trusted you and I care for you
but that doesn't seem to be enough
you're off to search for your soulmate
don't let me keep you from your fate.

CHAPTER 8

ARE YOU WAITING TO DUMP ON ME?

These feelings just won't go away
I'm resenting you're so far away
now I know you've never trusted me
haunting suspicions are overwhelming me.

You try and tell me you'll be true
but in my heart I'm doubting you
it's because of the things you did not say
until the call I did not make.

You went for me with a savagery
you clearly intended to damage me
I had a sense of déja vu
that I'd been down this road before.

Since then things have changed in me
I don't know what you want from me
I've trusted you without a doubt
now I sense danger all around.

Something has changed, I'm not sure what
it's to do with the way that you attacked
if I was there and you were here
I want to know, how would you act?

You've kept in contact with your past
I voiced my concerns, then trusted you
I'm not sure I can return to that
until there's one rule for me, and the same one for you.

CHAPTER 9
A QUESTION ASKED

I've loved you more than anyone
that I've loved in my life before
my commitment has been strong and true
which is more than I can say for you.

You tell me that I don't show for you
the feelings that I swear are true
but if you step back and look around
you'll see my feelings have been all too strong

If you can't believe me, ask your friends
and ask them what they think of me
and how they see the things I do
and what more do they think I could do for you.

If you ask me it's up to you
to understand the things you do
and to reason why you want to go
and cast our future to the wind.

CHAPTER 10

NOT DROWNING, I'M WAVING

She's a user, it's her style
she uses everyone she can
when she has what she has wanted
she moves on without a care.

You never tried to bridge the distance
between you and my two kids
you were happy just to leave them
they served no purpose for your needs.

You don't have to say it's over
I've been certain since last night
when I looked in you, for something true
and what I saw, was déja vu

I'll be strong and I feel certain
that someone waits for me to come
and I'll be there in all my glory
knowing my good deeds have come around.

So if you see me in the distance
arms waving frantic in the air
I'm not in a pool of tears of sadness
I'm just happy, I had my year.

CHAPTER 11
A TRUE LOVE VOW

While my sweetheart wears my ring
I pledge to play the waiting game
so remember the promise I made to you
whilst you wear my ring, that I'll be true.

I'll resist temptation great or small
I know you'll hear me if I fall
so in my heart time will stand still
until you come back, of your own free will.

CHAPTER 12

ME

Tomorrow brings a bright new day
I'll say my prayers and be on my way
to find my soulmate, and my destiny
the promised land that's awaiting me.

My journey has been long and hard
I've faced despair along the way
always with a sense of pride
that the things I did were not so bad.

Now I'll be led along the way
and now I can stop worrying
that my every move is filled with danger
take me to my waiting stranger.

Tonight I'll sleep a sleep of dreams
where peace and calm are on the breeze
and I feel sure that I'll be better
than I've ever been in my life before.

CHAPTER 13
MISSING YOU

Oh! yes how I'm missing you
the spark in my life-light for so long
now you're gone I feel so lonely
I want you back in my life right now.

The spirits tell me I must wait
till the time is right for you to say
that you've looked around and thought it through
and now you're sure that I'm the one for you.

This day can't come soon enough
I've waited a whole lifetime too,
to hold you close and hear you say
you miss me too, now you'll never let me go.

CHAPTER 14

HORSES TO WATER (OR, DID I SAY GOODBYE TONIGHT?)

Fran passed by from work tonight
we said hello, but did I say goodbye?
she sat and had a drink or two
we did not seem close, is that us through?

I ask these questions of myself
not knowing where the answers lie
sometimes I feel, we should be as one
then I look around, and again she's gone.

Maybe our time has passed
in a flash the spark was out
me, not quite knowing what had started it
or why it went from 'it' to shit.

I'm sure in time I'll work it out
how you can leave what we had behind
so when friends ask me I'll just say
even horses have to drink someday.

I feel I've woken from a dream
and I cannot say if we're in love
I don't know why I feel this way
did I say goodbye tonight?

CHAPTER 15
LETTING GO

Sometimes people try too hard
to be all things to every man
so much so they miss the point,
that what's best for them isn't best for you.

It's clear to me my time has passed
you are not here, because you don't want to be
and there's no point in asking why
It's a fact, I must let go.

You go and get on with your life
I know I'll stay within your heart
so on judgement day when you look back
you will remember me for evermore.

CHAPTER 16

I NEED TO KNOW

Tell me what you want of me
I need to see it with clarity
do you want us just to be friends
will we ever be lovers once again?

All the time I'm hanging on
to the dream that you'll be mine again
it's not fair, I do not know
what hope there is in your heart for us.

So tell me Fran, what do you want?
tell me honest and tell me true
do you want me at a distance,
or am I still there in your dreams?

CHAPTER 17
AN ULTIMATUM(?)

I do not want you just as a friend
be my wife or let us end
I love you too much to just stand around
until the time your prince has come.

It might be foolish to see in black and white
but I fear the way that it might end
we began the day that we first met
it ends the day you go with someone else.

That's the way it is with me
I want to be with you for eternity
and if on the day I die, I know you've been true
the rest of my life would have been lived for you.

CHAPTER 18
INTO THE SUNSET

As the sun sets on this love affair
I had wanted more than I could have
when the dream was lost, you did not cry
but I cried enough for both of us.

I could not wait for you to call
I listened to my inner voice
the one that makes me write these lines
the one saying, bring the curtains down.

I've suffered once again for art
that's the best way I can look at it
a poet writes from inspired thoughts,
thoughts that rise up from his heart.

So let's ride into the sunset now
as silhouettes on a fading skyline
tomorrow is another day
a new horizon is on the way.

 THE END.

MY PRAYER

Dear Lord, give me the strength, the courage,
And the wisdom, to follow the path of righteousness
That i can believe in you, so you can protect me,
And help me to remove all negativities
That undermine my self-confidence.
I pray that you hear my prayers
And guide me to the land of peace and tranquillity
I ask this in Jesus' precious name
Amen.

THE SINKING SUN.
(FOR FRAN - THE LAST GOODBYE)

I watched the sun sink in the sea
as a final act of this passing day
I felt a chill within my heart
as you performed your final act.

Didn't you know, I could be so cold?
when facing you, brazen and bold?
I did not want an acrimonious end
what could I do, you would not bend?

For the first three months, I faced the past
and after that, I kept looking back
and when I wanted to face ahead
you would not bring this to an end.

You went for broke, you wanted all,
everything that you had brought
there was no need to sink that low
because for my time with you, my cash just flowed.

I never took advantage of you
I never gave you troubled times
all I asked was that you paid your way
and for my crime you broke my heart.

I really thought so much of you
I would do everything that I could do
to keep you happy and keep you mine
but all the while you passed the time.

There was no need to end this way
we did not have that kind of love affair
I wanted to end as we had been
with pride and honour, kept intact.

But you brought it to this sorry end
where I'm asking for my presents back
for a man of honour and of truth
this is a degrading thing to do.

But I have to sink as low as you
to make sure I'm not being mugged
no one walks all over me
not if I have any say in it.

So I'll say goodbye and bid farewell
I do not wish any ill-will on you
I hope you have a happy life
and I hope you wish it for me too.

A BIRTHDAY ODE TO A PAST LOVE

Thinking of you on your birthday
I used to think we had it all
everything that I had wanted
could be found there in your arms.

You never said quite what it needed
to make you feel the same things too
maybe now that it is over
it will become clear to you.

I'm sure sometimes that you might wonder
why all we had, had turned to dust
remember, no one took my love from you
you chose to give it up for good.

If we ever had to end at all
I would rather that we ended this way
I would never want to hurt someone
and have them feel what I went through.

So happy birthday to you, Fran
I'll raise a glass and say a cheer
and wish you all the happiness
for today, tomorrow, and year on year.

ALL OUR YESTERDAYS

It felt so strange, to see you yesterday
the first time in so many months,
it felt like on my grave you were walking
the things you did, the way we were talking

But emotionally I have rebuilt that wall
and I cannot walk that road again
nevertheless it still feels weird
this visit from our yesterdays.

I'm sure you'll want to carry on
and stay in touch with me as friends
well, this will be a new one on me
I usually confine these things to history.

It remains the biggest disappointment in my life
the effort I gave, how I tried in vain
to make our relationship really work
even now I can still feel the pain.

So let's say goodbye to yesterday
and put our troubles far behind
I'll remember you for this summer's day
when we visited all our yesterdays.

A SAD ANNIVERSARY

It fills me with a sense of sadness
every time I think of you
it seems to me to be such a waste
did I ask too much of you?

This time last year, I was hurting so much
wanting you to stay with me
but you chose to go, and it made me cry
and all I could do, was to ask you why.

It's the nature of our personalities
that we had to end like this
I could not accept you as you were
and you would not compromise for me.

The distance between us wasn't great
but we could not take that leap of faith
to give to each other all we had
it just seemed a bridge too far.

I really feel it wasn't me
that brought it to a sorry end
I'm sure you feel the same way too
it's just that we weren't meant to be.

So it's a sad anniversary for me
although I'm as happy as I can be
I've really found my sense of peace
and I hope you've found your happiness.

MEMORIES OF A HAPPY TIME
(A BIRTHDAY ODE TO A PAST LOVE - 2)

I hope that when you think of me
they are memories of a happy time
when the dreams you had, when just a girl
seemed so near, when you held me close.

Something happened along the way
and we chose to go our separate ways
and for your second birth date since we parted
I write for you straight from the heart.

I've said before, and I know it's true
that I cannot walk that road again
too much water has passed our bridge
and memories I'll keep, locked in a fridge.

So happy birthday once again
and hope when you look back years from now
and remember what happened on your 30th,
they'll be memories of a happy time.

MORE WORDS

NADIA - A WOMAN FRIEND

Your strength and courage are clear to me
you love your man with devotion true
the cross you bear is tough, I see
yet your spirit shines on like a star.

You understand the gift of trust
to be alone, in a naked world
remaining calm and beyond temptation
to love your precious man, with true devotion.

I'm sure between the two of you
you can find the peace you hold so dear
and by the time your burden ends,
he'll appreciate how much you cared.

A STORY BOOK FOR ELIZE

(words to a granddaughter)

A fairy story to a child
Is like a world of dreams and fantasy
Where all the colours are so bright
Without a dark cloud in the sky.
But what you mean to us, my love
Is a future full of hope and joy
You are so cheeky, smart and bright
You fill our hearts and lift us up.
You are your parents' own fairy-tale.

from your granddad.

IT WAS A GOOD DAY TO DIE

(A tribute to my mother, 1934-1998)

Death, of which I never even think its name
in case it hastens its visit on the ones that I love.
Yet when yours came, as sudden as it was quick,
it was a release from all your fears and all your pains.

You lived your life in total faith,
to serve your god and spread his word,
your conviction was strong and true
as witnessed by all who knew you.

You gave me life and gave me hope,
Yes, all I am is down to you,
I try my best in all I do
because that is what I learnt from you.

I'm grateful for this passing year,
for the time I had to spend with you,
to do what I could to help you through
as you've done for me your whole life through.

My greatest thanks is for your death's timing,
you had a day that was heaven sent,
you spent your time on your ministry
then later at your kingdom hall.

I brought you home that Thursday night,
your spirit high and your mind at ease,
you called me through the bedroom wall,
as you'd done before in dreams gone by.

I went across to see what's wrong
and saw you sitting at the edge of the bed
you said to me, your head was hurting,
I knew right then, it was serious.

I called for help and talked to you
you did not cry, or show much fear,
you seemed to accept your time had come
and accepted death with dignity.

Your spirit and your soul live on
in your children's hearts and in their veins,
I know you held me in high esteem,
I felt the same about you too.

GOODBYE WATLING

(From Jim)

Goodbye Watling, I bid farewell
it's time to move to pastures new
in eight short years, the time has flown
now with every day, I recount a year.

We've seen some changes on the way
with computer screens, and a voice that calls
we've put carpets down and paint on walls
and central heating in the halls.

We've seen despair and tragedies
we've lost some friends along the way
but my lasting memories of Burnt Oak,
are my ready wit, and quick humour
with your warm response and smiles all round.

AKA Jim.

COME SEE THE PARADISE

(A song for whoever)

Come see the paradise
come share the dream
of two hearts together
in love supreme

come see the paradise
come see what I've got
a place you can run to
the place you forgot.

I can see in your eyes
that you still think of me
and it still is your loss
if you just let me go.

so look in the mirror
and ask yourself this -
what good has it done you
the chances you've missed?

So come see the paradise
stop hiding your dreams
you know that you want me
so come to me - please?

ALICE – ONE OF A KIND

(The strongest person I have known)

I wish that I could ease your pain
Of tragedies, to our families bring
As time goes by, and we get older
They multiply, and leave us colder.

Of all the years that I have known you
You've kept your feeling deep inside you
Now to lose a child at this time
You must feel the world's against you.

Yet throughout the times that I have known you
Your strength and courage has been all about you
I've never known someone so strong
You've led your family from the front.

So Alice, keep your spirits up
And remember just how much we love you
There is hope and comfort in your children's eyes
And a bright future in their children's lives.

ALL ROADS LEAD TO ROME

I do not know where this road leads
and I step with caution at every turn
I know that you are with someone
but this road may yet lead to Rome.

I have looked for signs along the way
that that's not where you want to be
but you keep your cards close to yourself
is this out of loyalty?

What do you see when you look at me?
are you seeing what I can see?
do you ever dream of me?
am I in your fantasy?

If you answer yes at any time
and if thoughts of me just fill your mind
and if you wonder why that is
maybe this road leads to Rome.

(TO NAD)

I want to hold you

Last night I dreamt I held you close
and whispered sweet words in your ear
it felt to me like you responded
and all our fears just disappeared.

We have pledged that we'll be honest
not so much in many words
we just know that you're committed
to fulfil your pledge of truth.

I won't be the one to push you
into something, that you might regret
anyway, I don't need it
not the complicated grief I'll get.

so we'll keep each other at a distance
and hope these feelings come to pass
because I don't know how long I can see you
if I cannot hold you close.

A ONE-NIGHT STAND(?)

What is in a one-night stand?
what is there to understand?
will it satisfy our lustful greed?
what about your emotional needs?

We like to feel that we are free
to choose to do with each other as we please
we can even say we knew before
the dangers of a swinging door.

Now here we are, it feels so strange
not knowing what is coming next
not quite sure, just what to do
to make this thing run smoothly through.

What thing is this? I hear you ask
what way can we run with it?
I really don't know what to say
because your problem will not just go away.

I do not want to hurt anyone
not you, not me, not anyone
I only want a happy life
for you, for me, for everyone.

AN IMPOSSIBLE DREAM(?)

I want to thank you Nad, for giving back to me
my self-belief and confidence
there was a time when I wasn't sure
that I could be the man I was before.

You've given me that ray of hope
that one day soon, I'll find that dream
where peace and love comes hand in hand
and there are no dragons from behind.

With you there's only half that dream
I just cannot stop my worrying
knowing there's a storm to come
with dangerous fall outs all around.

I really don't know what to do
should I sacrifice what I've found with you
I know I can't go on this way
without a plan for the way ahead.

My head tells me, it has to end
can we go back to just being friends?
you'll have the choice to come back to me
if you can find a way out of this tragedy.

You said that it would be up to me
to make a choice as to what to do
I really don't know what I should do
and I think that it is up to you.

CHOOSE ME (TO NADIA)

If you take your time, and think it through
the choice is really up to you
you know exactly where I stand
I'm ready and waiting to be your man.

The choice you face is no choice at all
because you've sacrificed so much so far
and in return what have you had?
veiled threats, for being bad.

I stand before you as the man
you've dreamt about your whole life through
and you are the one that I would choose
when I take my time, and think it through.

so choose me Nad, and we'll make it work
do what's in your best interest
put yourself first, and do what's right
and tell me I'll be yours tonight.

YOUR PRINCE HAS COME

I long to say the things I feel
with you I think I can find that dream
it's clear to me, we can be a team
once you can find a way to end with him.

Could you grab the tiger by the tail?
are you sure enough to face his rage?
how else can we get ahead
and be your own person, and not his slave?

He'll have to know your prince has come
with me, that you have found someone
who brings the sunshine through your day
and shines you a light for the way ahead.

It's not your fault you fell in love
in a perfect world, you would have cleared your decks
but fate has brought us together now
we can't change time, so let it flow.

You've known for years that it wasn't him
you've tried your best to be his
but in your heart, you know you could never be
everything he wants you to be.

But with me you know it feels so right
why should you let this chance pass you by?
will you ever get another chance to say
for this lifetime, my prince will stay?

TO LEAD A DOUBLE LIFE

Can you lead a double life
from now until the end of his time?
can we carry on our way?
whilst you still have other calls to pay?

It's only time before something gives
either you'll be seen with me
or your timing might not be so right
it's then we'll have to face this fight.

we cannot talk of the things we feel
because there's no point even if you're sure
you'll have to put that ghost away
and let us begin along our way.

That won't be an easy thing to do
and we're not going to let each other go
but somehow, some way, it has to end
this double life you seem to lead.

I'll give you time, and I'll give you space
but the conclusion will still be the same
you can't be mine, when he dictates to you
I feel I'm not protecting you.

So think about it for a while
think about the things you want
see what's standing in your way
then make a choice for my heart to stay.

IF YOU CAN LET ME GO

If you can let me go right now,
then this thing wasn't really meant to be
and if there's one lesson I have learned
I won't waste my time trying the tide to turn.

For you I know it's hard and tough
to have to face this kind of stress
but the choice you make to serve your time
is yours alone, make no mistake.

I've shown you there's another way
to lead your life in peace and calm
but you cannot take that faithful step
to close the door, on this waste of time.

Think for a moment what he would do
if he was standing in your shoe
if you were there and he was here
are you really sure that he would care?

Well anyway, I've had my say
if you want me to, then I can stay
but if you can let me go right now
then I can only walk away.

But if I stay you must be sure
and there will be no turning back
you'll be my wife, and we'll lead our lives
for each other, and our cares.

THE ROAD FROM HELL

Get ready for that judgement day you face
you can't ride two horses in one race
your destiny is to be with me
we blend into each other seamlessly.

Your life with him must be a living hell
how can you plan your day ahead?
you must be indoors come what may
to take his calls five times a day.

He resents you going out to work
yet still you have to pay his way.
He resents your skirt on a summer's day
and blames you if anyone looks your way.

When you're with me you can be yourself
you don't have to watch the things you say
I know, you know, we can be as one
or you can choose to stay with the devilish one.

The road from hell is never smooth
You'll need strength and courage along the way
and I'm here to guide you all the way
remember every dog will have his day.

We have started and we have carried on
to take some steps along the way
when the bomb explodes I'll be standing there
to protect you and you'll know I care.

PRELUDE TO A CONVERSATION

When I saw you standing there,
I sat rooted to my chair
I felt right then there was an attraction
the way you moved, the way we stared.

I'm sure I'll ask "what do you want?"
you've already asked me "what do you do?"
what this seem to me to be
is a prelude to a conversation.

SO CLOSE TO HEAVEN

If you are what I see
and you can come to me
then my world will be complete
and I will live the rest of my life
for you.

THE SPIRIT OF ITALIA

The spirit of Italia is with me
the land of romantics and of poetry,
the sun, the sea, and our chemistry
and thoughts of you, and what it could be.

I'm sad, but glad that I am leaving Rimini
because I know we could never be
and to gaze day after day at your beauty
I am sure it would end up killing me.

I hope sometime you might remember me
as the stranger from across the sea
who came to visit your Italy
for the culture, art, and the scenery.

We came to play in a football tour
but when I looked at you, I saw much more
Patricia, you are so beautiful
that memories of Italia will be with me, for ever more.

IT'S JUST THE WAY WE WERE

(Utopian love is still a dream)

For me Utopian love is just a dream
a dream I've lost along the way.
When I think of all the loves I've lost
there was nothing I could have changed to make them stay.

Yet none are speaking ill of me
and they seem to want their time again
and for Fran I feel a sense of sadness
because I know our time has passed us.

I've come to terms with what I am,
a thoughtful person, who likes himself
I would not choose to be anyone else
I'm just glad for being me.

I've thought it through, and I've worked it out
eternal love was never meant to be
with mankind's greed and selfishness
means we'll always be wanting more, not less.

When I think of how I felt back then
and I really felt I had lost my way
it was just that I had expected more
of human trust, than there was to give.

Philosophers have known since time
that betrayal is part of the human form
and every page of history
is littered with broken hearts and promises.

But that's what makes us what we are
to be strong and to start again
always being positive
because Utopian love is still my dream.

TO ANNIA

an autumn's dream.

It would be nice, to choose the time
to meet someone you could call 'mine'
and to pick someone that fits the bill
who knows you well, and gives you a thrill.

But that's the nature of relationships
they often start, when you first meet
whatever circumstances might be
you've met me now, so we will see.

You have the choice, to be with me
or let me go, and you can stay free
so it's entirely up to you
to choose to do what's best for you.

For me there is no choice to make
I would go with you, if you wanted me to
and if you don't, it would be a shame
because in some ways, we are the same.

So Annia it is up to you
to tell me what you want to do
I can be a friend, but I want much more
to be your man, and your lover too.

TO CLAIRE - SHOULD I GO THERE?

Did you swoon, when you first saw me?
I was taken aback when I looked at you.
It felt like it was a summer's breeze,
which soon turned into a winter's freeze.

I don't know what to make of us
I thought I would leave it up to you
to choose to go where you wanted to
if you led the way, I would follow too.

It seems to me that you don't want to
I can assure you that's all right by me
but still there, something lingers on
and I would not want to miss the chance of your 'come-on'.

So tell me Claire, should I go there?
or take my leave, back to my chair,
back to the calm and peace of my humdrum life
sensing romantic adventure is around the corner.

CLAIRE

I don't know

I don't know why I should feel so anxious
I don't know why I should feel scared
I have this thought, I think about you
but I can't think it through to a natural end.

It's not that I don't have the courage
it's not that I can't face the truth
it's only that you need to show me
that something stirs within you too.

I don't know if it's time to ask you
if you really feel for me
I'm asking myself the same question
what do I really feel for you?

I don't know where this thought is going
I don't know where it's going to end
I only know I want you near me
and now is the time to tell you so.

A DREAM COME TRUE

(Let's go for it)

Now that we have found each other
will we ever let it go?
from the things that we've been saying
somehow, I just don't think so.

I sense that you and I are thinking,
seeing, dreaming the same things
just to be as one together
living, sleeping, in the same dream.

It's nice to know we've found each other
it's nice to think, we're going for it.
it's nice to be so sure of the future
it's nice to feel it was meant to be.

So come on Eunice, talk to me
tell me that you know it's true
tell me I'm the one you've wanted
and now your dreams are coming true.

THANKING YOU

(For Eunice)

If I can say 'thank you' for being you,
it really understates the things I mean
my heart, it feels so full to burst
it feels so right, just loving you.

We've come together, with no intent
and we've known each other, with some content
yet all we did was to take a look
and we've found in each other the things we sought.

It feels to me like we're meant to be
because the things you feel, when you're holding me
and the thoughts I have, when I'm missing you
mean I just have to keep seeing more of you.

So thank you Eunice, for being you
for being here, and for being there
for wanting me, like I'm wanting you
and for making all my dreams come true.

A LOVE UNDERSTATED

(Utopian love pt. 2)

I don't have to tell the world about it
I don't have to say the way I feel
I only know that now I'm with you
there's nowhere else I'd rather be.

It's been so long since I first wished for
someone with whom I could share a dream
to be to each other, all we longed for
that 'Utopian love' which was my dream.

Eunice, you don't have to say you love me
and I don't have to say to you
all the things that I am feeling
because I know you feel them too.

It's just so nice, to be together
always in each other's thoughts
knowing now, we've found each other
our love from here, will only grow.

TO DREAM THE IMPOSSIBLE DREAM

(Utopian love part 3)

I start to think the impossible dream
when thoughts of you come to my mind
it seem a stupid thing to do
to think a wish, that you'll soon be mine.

But start the dream? indeed I have
and my pounding heart is beating faster
to be with you, all my dreams come true.
can this wonderful thing ever be real?.

The obstacles we'll have to pass
and I don't even know, what's in your heart
but the way you speak, and when you're next to me
make me want to be with you.

Yet still it seems impossible
our circumstances, our age difference
it seems so wrong, because you're so young
Yet I sense you've had that dream yourself.

If you feel anything for me
or thoughts of me, occupy your mind
and if you want to be with me,
just say the word, and you'll be mine.

I NEED TO KNOW

(Utopian love pt. 4)

What is it about you
that's driving me insane?
why can't I forget you
instead of wanting to be with you again?

This isn't just a sex thing,
or to recapture my youth again
This is something deeper
that's unsettling me again.

Every time I think of you,
it begins and ends the same
it starts with wanting to be with you
and ends with "no" again.

Yet every time I see you,
I can't be drawn away
it doesn't seem to affect you
do you understand my pain?

I've told myself, I will not show
just what I feel inside
for any of it to matter
you will have to feel the same.

I cannot make you love me
I cannot force your care
I can only wish you'd see me
as the man to make you dare.

I really believe, if I were with you
all my dreams would come true.
It's just something about you
I would risk everything for you.

I really did not want to say
all I feel inside
unless/until you had showed to me
you felt something for me too.

I really want to show to you
all I can be to you
I'd hope you'd look at everything
it could be really good for you.

All there is, is the age difference
and our current circumstance
but in my mind, there is no fear
and my conscience now is really clear.

So will you come and take a chance
and be my "one true love"?
and every day I spend with you
I will be thanking god.

ONLY WHEN I SEE HER

(A Forlorn Lover's Tale)

Pulses race, hearts embrace
Thinking of you through the day
A heart's desire, in lust of fire
Common sense flew out the window.

It only happens when I see you
My senses, feelings, touch are heightened
I'll take a risk and take the chance
To show you how I feel about you.

Yet all I do is taint with caution
I try to hide the things I am feeling
But every time that I have seen you
I've ended feeling sad again.

Now as time flies and I don't see you
And I come back down to earth again
I think more clearly, and I can see reason
Until I see you once again.

STRANGERS IN OUR PRIVATE WORLD

(Will we ever have that conversation?)

There's so much that is left unspoken
So many things we haven't said
It's very strange, the way we've acted
We've never had that private word.

Still when you act, I have reacted
And I can sense what you are thinking
Yet not a word of it we've spoken
Except a 'Freudian slip' by me.

I know what is best for me
To stay away, and stop that lusting
To listen to my head, which clearly warns me
And I feel sure you feel the same.

So will we ever have that conversation
Where we can talk about how brave we've been?
Or to stay clear, of each other
Fearing where that talk will lead.

THINKING OF YOU

I can't help but think about you
Can't help but wanting to be with you
It seems like every time we meet
It reminds me how I felt for you.

It was nice to see your smile again
When I looked in your eyes, I saw a flame
Last night you really felt so close
If I could only find a way, to make you say…

To make you say, I will be your man
And to you I will always be true
Just you standing next to me
We looked so cool, I felt hot for you.

Now all I do is think of you
Should I call you up, or wait in vain?
Or wait until the next time we meet
And let you know just how I feel?

REQUIEM FOR A SELFLESS MAN
(A tribute to Pantalis Georgiou)

How can I begin to tell
of your selflessness to everyone?
your care and kindness knew no bounds
you were the same to everyone.

Now in the twilight of your life
with fate dealing you a crucial blow
the cancer that is hurting you
can't stop your courage shining through.

Pantalis, with a heart of gold
you gave your all to everyone
it's hard to describe the man you are
for someone so kind, it's very rare.

So I say a little prayer for you
and pray to God to send a cure
to make you better, and get what you deserve
just enjoying the nature of our world.

A BIG THANK YOU!
(MY TAKE ON IT)

To Richard and all concerned (saying something profound)

I want to thank you all for giving me the chance
to share in one of life's great dreams
A great adventure, like no other
as a winner in one of your schemes.

I feel blessed to have experienced
some of the adventures I have seen
To fete with lords and presidents
is more than I can take in.

I have to pinch myself, to believe it's real
The things that I have seen
I watched with mirth, as my son saw death
in the jaws of the shark's revenge.

Thanks for the chance to show my son
just what hard work can bring
not just in cash terms, but spiritually too
because I had the chance to pay a tribute.

Thanks for the chance to see the place
where the heroes of my race
with dignity and inhuman strength
showed humankind the way to go.

I would not have missed it for the world
The adventures I have had,
the friends I've made, the fun we've had
the bonds that we have made.

It was wonderful to work so hard,
and rewarded with such kindness
I'll tell my friends and all work colleagues
you too can have the same.

AKA James

AN UNUSUAL PLACE TO BE

I know how we got to there,
but I don't know where we go from here
it's as if it's like it used to be
it's as if there is no history.

If it did not happen, and I was wrong
if you did not react the way you had done
if I had no sorrows, from your slings and arrows
then I would know what to make of our tomorrows.

This is an unusual place to be
for someone as logical as me
we seem to have gone from A to C
without a thought as to what will be.

I had to find another way
so I went back to the start again
I can't forget what I have seen
I can't pretend it's never been.
How can we even find a peace?
when you believe what I cannot see
and you can't see, what is clear to me
my only truth, is what I believe.

I don't have the will, and don't have the heart
to start a fight to a bitter end
but I can't pretend everything is well
and I can't pretend that I'm content.

I'm not in control of my destiny
at least that's how it feels to me
it feels as if I have no say
I hope fate will show me the right way.

CAST ADRIFT FROM THE ANCHOR OF TRUST

(An unusual place to be pt. 2)

Cast adrift from solid ground
I cannot find a peace of mind
time and chances have gone by
are we still the trusting kind?

I'm standing still, from yesterday
where I witnessed what you had to say
to say I was shocked and hurt by you
is understating the whole truth.

You showed a fragile state of mind
where fears and unhappiness would thrive
your anger was hysterical
your hate and hostility, tangible.

Now it seems that none of this was true
as we amble on, with what seem like togetherness
yet cast adrift, from the rock of trust
I need the strength to carry on.

My fears are getting in the way
to break the link and start again
my thoughts are turning cynical
and negative and critical.

Will I ever find my dream?
or settle for what's clearly not
what I think true love should be
full of trust, a oneness and a togetherness.

FOUR SEASONS (THE LONG GOODBYE)

Back in the fall, I got a call,
my senses sounding messages
I sensed the wind of change again
there had to be a reason.

I braced myself, and cleared my mind
and watched it all unravel.
I lamented that I had done my best
but for you, there was something missing.

The winter came with festive fare
and at Christmastime we settled
but on New Year's Eve you made the move
that proved to be decisive.

I did not stop you when you said
you wanted to go dancing
I did not cry, when you chose your friends
and left me on my lonesome.

I reasoned that you wanted out
I said so in the kitchen,
I told my friend, it was the end
or at least it seemed so to me.

The spring approached and things got worse
you started taking chances.
You kept away to make your play
and kept me at a distance.

I realised the time had come
to read the writing on the wall
I made my choice, and I chose out
but I tried to guide you through it.

For you it seemed I was so wrong
and you could not see my reasons
there was no way you'd let me go,
I had to make a decision.

Now summer's here, and I have faced my fears
and I'm grappling with the nettles
if I learn in time, that I should have changed my mind,
I'd still settle for my reasons.

I CANNOT MAKE YOUR DREAM COME TRUE

(Why I had to go)

Your focus changed in recent times
you seem to have found a different light
a chance to make your dream come true
a chance to raise two girls - like you.

The past two weeks have told a tale
of where your heart's desire lay
it troubled me, I took the blame
for your stress and anger and unhappiness.

When I saw you on Thursday night,
you did not have a thing to say
you did not want to say too much
though I had not seen you, in six days.

I realised our time had come
to deal with the problems in your mind
here I stand, right in the way
of something to make your dream come true.

For years you've wanted to be 'mum' to girls
and right now you are doing that
you're doing fine, and are loving it
but at a stroke, it could be gone from you.

That isn't what you're dreaming of
and isn't what is happening
in fact you're playing families
and I'm just standing in the way.

I asked you, in the past two weeks
how much time I had spent with you,
I hadn't seen you very much
about four or five times, at the most.

I asked you "in the past two weeks"
how often had you seen Jason,
it turned out almost every day
and sometimes he even stayed for tea.

It seems to me, you've made your choice
of where you see your future lay,
and to get to there, I will have to go
because I'll be standing in your way.

I don't feel bad, just a little sad
we've had good times along the way
but when you told me of the day you've had
I was getting in the way.

It was past twelve when you came in
you did not have a thing to say
I had not seen you in six days
that told me, I was in the way.

For the three years I have been with you
I gave to you what you couldn't give
the freedom to be your natural self
a freedom only love and trust can bring.

Now you have to face your truth
of what it is you want from me
you cannot tell it like it is
you know I'm standing in your way.

THIS IS WHY, THIS IS GOODBYE

I did not want to hurt your feelings
I don't want to make you blue
it's just that I can't ignore my instincts
that tell me it is time to go.

The life we've led in recent times
is not the way it used to be
and when I look at all the reasons
it worked out, it was meant to be.

When your heart is full, and you have that hunger
to be with me your whole life through
you cannot see, that what's just happened
is a brighter future, for you too.

I really don't want to put you through it
and I really know your pain inside
there is no way, when love is ending
that you can hide that hurt inside.

This is the story of my lifetime
this endless search for my one true love
I really sense it has to happen
before I run right out of time.

If I had looked, right at the beginning
it would have been, so plain to see
even for you, there was something missing
that 20%, to make your dream come true.

So Eunice, though we are still together
sharing the hurt we're going through
but I sense, that when it's over
we will both be happy for seeing it through.

When you look at what really happened
how the distance really grew
because I knew I could not be better
it was time to push on through.

I really feel it was in your subconscious
to bring this journey to an end
because I know I would not betray you
I will not wait for a bitter end.

It is time to find that someone
that fate has chosen, for me to love
I don't know if I'll ever find her
but somewhere she waits, for me to come.

because I'm sure, you've thought about it
when you had doubts, that I was the one
you've probably thought, what I am thinking
that very soon, your prince will come.

WITNESS TO A TAVERN BRAWL

The most savage act I have ever seen.
(as I walked on by the other side)

I went for a pint on Sat'day night
as we always do when Rangers are home
we sat in the Prince and had a chat
with a West Ham fan, we chatted away.

There were five lads sat across the way
with their macho banter, and fighting talk.
Everything was jolly and seemed so calm
as we waited for Khan v Salita.

There was a shriek - a scream, from the other side
a female's voice, so full of fire
it was someone I had known before,
the sister of a friend I had had a relationship with.

What the row was about, no one could tell
as she threw a stool across the room
there were so many peacemakers, trying to calm her down
she would not have it, she was havin' it.

My gut instinct was to stay away
away from harm, I could see coming
then her husband, he came into view
demanding to know, what was going on.

It seemed two lads, had upset her
they were friends of the five, stood in the corner
Karen seemed hell bent for war
her fighting head, she really had it on.

What happened next, is still shocking me
she provoked a lad, out with his dad
he struck the first blow at her husband
and then the next, and the next, as Karen grabbed a glass.

(The attack on her husband carried on
despite the fact he was not fighting
the sheer weight of numbers, was too much
for any one person to be fighting.)

She was disarmed and shoved away
she came back strong, and smashed a bottle
right on top of that lad's head
then hell was let loose - someone could have died tonight.

They set about her, three grown men
the father, his mate, and another one
the father he kicked her full in the face
as she lay sickened, on the ground.

I have never witnessed such violence
against a stricken woman, lying on the floor
I knew that if I intervened
I would face the same violence.

No one should ever be treated that way
with so much violence, and hostile hate
she lay on the floor, so full of pain
as I stood by on the other side.

I feel so ashamed, to have witnessed this
but I know why, I did not act
I would have put my life at risk
and what would I have been dying for?

Somewhere in the midst of this
Ray went outside to have a fag
where he witnessed the restraining arms, of one of them
as the flashing blade showed the other's intent.

if I had moved I would have been attacked
I would have tried to defend myself
if they had met any resistance
they would have used, the tools they carried.

My gut instinct was to stay away
my sixth sense warned me, not to be brave
to use my head and to stay clear
from the horrors that would have surely followed.

So I walked on by the other side
I faced another test of my character,
I was not brave, gallant, or showed any chivalry
but I am still alive to tell the tale.

THE SWEETNESS OF YOUR SMILE - (I WILL REMEMBER)

A tribute to Susan Conway, RIP

The first thing when I think of you,
was the sweetness of your smile
when I heard the news, you had passed away,
I was in shock, and in great sadness.

Your husband Pat, and your two sons
God, how I really feel for them
to lose someone so young, so dear
their pain must be immense.

With a heart of gold, where kindness flowed
the soft melody of your voice,
the thing I will remember most
was the sweetness of your smile.

The happy aura that you wore
reminds me of summers past
with the kindest of souls and a king-size heart
Susan, you really lit up this world.

It's really sad to think you're gone
and I won't see you again
but tonight heaven is a brighter place
for the sweetness of your smile.

WORDS - FROM THE BOSS THAT WOULD BE FAIR

All the time we've spent together
is more than we share with those at home
so much of our working lifetime
is spent with those we did not choose.

Yet all of this we have to manage
to get along, the best we can
and even when there is a fall out
we have to work harder to get along.

It's nearly four years we've been together
some happy times along the way
I've tried to make each day a good one
and have some fun along the away.

Each of you can think of some time
when you've felt hurt by something I've said
the words I've used to hit the target,
were only said because the spot was there.

so if you may have felt my style of management
to treat you all in an open forum,
with respect and care, but sometimes hurtful.
for this I must apologize, I never mean to hurt anyone.

So some time in the distant future
when you look back, or if you're ever asked of me
what do you remember of James the manager?
I hope you'll say - 'he was the boss that would be fair'.

COME AND BE MY LOVE

(Let's make our dreams come true if it's really meant to be)

I have been searching, more than your whole lifetime
to find that special someone, that was meant for me.
our paths first crossed, in two thousand and four
we did not know it then,
but surely it was meant to be.

Four years went by, and I did not see you
I did not know if you ever thought of me
but when I saw you, in two thousand and eight
you acted like you really missed me,
was it really meant to be?

Six months later, then we worked together
there must have been something that triggered me
I took a big risk, and asked to see you
but you rejected me! with much hostility
maybe it was not meant to be.

I told you I would not be trying
to upset you, or call again
until now - the time of our reckoning
I have to try, this one last time
to find out if it was really meant to be.

I cannot say what I have been feeling
it would only matter if you felt the same
the hand of fate has led me to this

now all of it is up to you to prove,
if it was really meant to be.

So take a chance to look at my love
you know I will always take care of you
you may feel the years between us
are too much for someone like you to bear
well that is a test - if it was really meant to be.

Yet if you look at me the way that you see me
and forget the tales of old father time
and look into your heart, what you have been feeling
do you really want to live your life without me?

So come and be my love, come and live your life
the way you have dreamt that it really could be
I believe that you love me, though you have never told me
think what you would feel, to live your life
without me in it....

IT IS ONLY A PHOTOGRAPH(S)

(2013 - reflections of the times gone by)

It fills me with a teary sadness
reflecting on the times gone by
all the times I had forgotten
brought back by a photograph.

All the things I have experienced
and with all the lessons that I have learnt
that a lifetime comes and go so quickly,
reflected by my photographs.

For sixteen years, I have not seen them
stored away in a loft somewhere
and now they're here, to bring back memories
and reflections of my times gone by.

All my life, I have looked forward
carrying the test of time,
now looking back, with all my photos
my sense of peace, I've truly earned.

PAST LOVES

HELLO AGAIN!

I remembered your eyes, but did not recognise you

PART 1

Some sweet stranger passed me by,
I did not take much notice,
then she came and spoke to me
I remembered her eyes,
but I did not recognise you.

So many years have passed us by
when we were young and carefree
you asked my name and said to me
you had always thought about me.

I was stunned, and said to you
you were right there in my memories
there was a romantic haze when I had thought of you
but I had not done so in ages.

As I looked at you, it all came back
when I had held you close that morning
you were so sweet and oh! so shy
I remembered your eyes,
but I had not recognised you.

HELLO AGAIN!
PART 2

So we said hello and talked about
the times that we remembered
then I said to you, I would go with you
if you would come along with me.

You said no, at least not yet
you would not go in a hurry
so I smiled inside, I was your 'brave white knight'
yet your heart seemed frightened of me.

I remembered then, as it was back then
how our story never got started
I had wanted you, but did not know how
to get you to trust in me.

So we went our ways, until today
when you passed sweetly by me
I'll remember your eyes as they gazed at me
Why didn't I recognise you?

HELLO AGAIN!

PART 3

(What if we were to fall in love?)

So we took the chance to look again
at our history, and the choice we made
we went back to that place of dreams
as we looked at what we have become.

It's clear to me that what I feel
and what you think, are just the same.
As if we could just stand outside
and take our leave, when trouble came.

But what if we were to fall in love
like the things I feel when holding you?
and what if I have lived up to
the way you've always thought of me?

Can we turn our backs again?
and have too many things got in the way?
can either of us stay away
from what we've missed for many years?

We'll take our time, and find our way
to where we know we have to be
to do what's in our best interests
and I'll do what I think is right for me.

I'm sure that you will do the same
but I'm not sure where we go from here
the next few weeks will tell a tale
we'll find out what is in our fate.

HELLO AGAIN!
PART 4

(The good, the bad and the angry/ugly)

There's three aspects to this relationship,
three things as I can see
this is a roller-coaster ride
the good, the bad and the ugly.

The good is when I'm holding you
or even sitting down together,
to have a chat, and have a laugh
and the feelings we remembered.

The bad is our circumstance
when we are not together,
when we cannot speak, and you cannot call
because to someone else you're tethered.

Angry is the way you get
when I cannot be bothered
to get out of my bed at night
to see you to the door.

The ugly is the way you are
when you just can't be bothered,
to tell me that you've changed your plans
and turn it to my misdemeanour.

I really have to laugh out loud
when I stop to think about it,
here I am, kept in the dark
and it's all my own fault really.

HELLO AGAIN! ...AND GOODBYE.

Part 5 (the unravelling)

Although it seemed our time had passed
we stopped to take another look
and what we've seen has come to this
the outcome was inevitable.

If you ask me how it came to be,
I'll answer with two questions
just ask yourself, what was it I said
and why I came to say it.

The answer is, it's what you want
I read the writing on the wall
you said a lot, and I thought out loud
and we said goodbye forever.

It was interesting to go back there
where our senses were rekindled
we felt the things we crave for most
but always with restrictions.

It proved to me that I was right
there can only be two people
in any one relationship
and three is doomed to failure.

So I'll say farewell, and wish you well
and I'm sure you will remember
that people do what's best for them
and this is what we chose to do.

THE SADDEST DAY

(what became of the broken-hearted)
(a tribute to Bernadette, RIP September 2006

I had the saddest news today
a girl I had loved had passed away
I had spoken to her, just the other day
she had buried her twin, who had passed away.

Whenever we spoke, she would let me know
I was the one, and she had let me go
she had told me once, how she would sit and weep
as she held my pictures, and played my tapes.

I will always remember how I felt back then
with my broken heart, when we had ended
I had loved her so, with all my heart
I wrote and told her how I felt
in words and letters, that I've kept today.

Bernadette was a true love in my life
a major milestone for my heart
I believed I could never love again
I could not reason why we parted.

A few years back, she called me up,
and we talked about how our lives had gone
it was clear to me she would live for me
if I could go back there again.

I could not forget the pain I'd lived
and I would not go back there again.
I felt sad to let her down,
I was only thinking of my own interests.

The walk we took down memory lane
rekindled hopes of a love affair;
what really, really makes me sad
one word from me, and she'd be whole again.

Now you've gone and died this way
alone at home for several weeks
I wish I had brought you happiness
instead of dying alone with a broken heart.

A BIRTHDAY ODE TO A RECENT LOVE

Happy birthday Eunice-May
yes, it's that time of year again
as you look back on a summer past
and wish for a more successful year.

I hope you've found your sense of peace
and the freedom, just to be yourself
you deserve some happiness
for all you've done for everyone.

OUR SISTER

(Her body's weak, but her spirit strong)

It feels so sad, to see you this way
it fills me up, and I hurt for you
you had health and strength, just the other day
life can be cruel, it hits you this way.

Now you're back, we'll take care of you
time to focus on your road to health
we'll take it slow and face day by day
your goal ahead, your place in the sun.

If anyone can make it true
everyone knows it must be you
your spirit and your will to win
have stood the test of time, more battles still.

If there's anything that I can do
just say the word, and I'll be true
I'll pray for you, and have faith in you
to make sure all of our dreams come true.

FAMILIES

Lies, deceit and betrayal

IN PRAISE OF SARAH

(you make me proud)

I wish there was more that I could do
to stop this pain you're going through
but I'll do all I can to guide you through
your courage and your strength will do the rest.

This is the worst time in your life
you do so much for everyone
how could someone hurt you so
when you gave up your childhood for him?

I know in time you will be fine
you are so strong, you do not know
the crosses you have had to bear
for one so young, that's serious.

As a pregnant child you pulled him up
you gave him strength and he leaned on you.
you made a home and a family
now he's thrown it all away for free.

I know in time he'll feel your pain
when the boot will be on the other foot
you'll remember the hurt you're going through
and I know you will come shining through.

THE MASTER OF DECEIT

Saying goodbye to yesterday

A little lie can start the tear
that brings a waterfall
you've told a million lies thus far
yet you swear, it was the truth.

The hurt you bring didn't mean a thing
to you and your dear mum,
to add to the pain you gave, you have no shame
you kicked your daughter in the teeth.

So I'll say goodbye to yesterday
and when I think of you,
I'll remember your lies, and your deceit
and you - the master of deception.

I gave my life, and I gave my all
to make a life with you
I trusted you, then I needed you
how could you be so cruel?

Today I see a light ahead
and I know what I must do
I will confine you to history
in a deep permafrost.

So I'll say goodbye to yesterday
and when I think of you,
I'll remember your lies and your deceptions,
and you - the master of deceit.

TO SARAH

'The Strength Of Your Forgiveness'
(I Think I've Walked This Path Before)

Who can say they'll never sacrifice,
everything for love, without dignity, and even more?
and who can say they would never seek to destroy,
the one they loved, if they burnt a trust?

It's easy just to stand outside
and make a judgment, just like that
but who knows what it feels inside
unless you've walked that path before?

A betrayal of trust can kill someone
destroying the fabric of so many lives
but this is such a human trait
by now we should have got used to it.

But no, we stand on sermon high
saying 'never would I act this way'
sure enough it's been done to me
but I would never do that to you again.

So look in the mirror and cast no stone
you can be strong and walk away
leaving shattered dreams and lives behind
and start the quest for love again.

Or we can be strong in another way
and look to find the things we crave
to be at peace, and to be in love
with respect and with care,
just with the strength of your forgiveness.

TO RICHARD

**you can pass the test of time.
(a personal message)**

To have gone to the edge of darkness
then thrown yourself at mercy's door
you have shown tremendous courage
please don't throw it all away.

The strength and courage it must have taken
to expose your fears to hostile foes,
and the only thing that you have asked for
was the chance to show you really cared.

Although it seems the whole world hates you
this is not how it really is
everyone has their fears of darkness
you can't control theirs, deal with your own.

The only thing that really matters
is how you feel about each other
you can't control how others treat you
all you can do is to be yourself.

I have seen your true commitments
to make amends, and show you care
Richard Shaw, I salute you
if you could only see how brave you've been.

You have to be true, to the things you treasure
your daughters' love, and Sarah's care
you're the only one she wants to be with
so don't hurt yourself, you both deserve better.

TO HAILEY

A story about life
(everything changes, yet everything stays the same)

Hindsight is a wonderful thing
we can make the changes that seemed so right
we can look again at the choices we made
that led us up an alleyway.

Yet the choices we made were set for us
our moral instinct led the way
our truth to us was set in stone
but with hindsight, was it all it seemed?

If you look back at your history
and the story of your life so far
with the dramas that you face today
this scenario has been played before -
with a different role for each of us.

Whether villain, victim or supporting act
these issues really are the same
with a different viewpoint, how right we were
yet wrong to hurt the ones we love.

I have lived this all before
I've been vilified, and have been full of hate
the slings and arrows I have faced,
for Richard, it is just the same.

It's the reactions of the human race
for retribution, and for punishment.
the hate-filled venom that's been expressed
seemed justified, from where they stood.

So I ask you please to look again
what really is the point you make?
to punish your sibling, for being human-kind?
or to help and support her, through her pain?

TO LAURRIE

'To be your father's daughter'
(treat others as they have treated you)

There's nothing wrong to sacrifice yourself,
to even make a foe of your father's will
just be sure it's for a worthy cause
and not act like an imbecile, for others, more evil.

For whom will it be, this self-sacrifice?
how did you choose, your most worthy one?
for a friend, kin, or even a sibling?
this wondrous person, what have they ever done for you?

For clarity, you should make a list
write on one side, from their goodwill, what have they ever done for you?
and on the other side, when you have needed them,
did they stand for you, or did they walk by on the other side?

Be true to yourself, and face your facts
not some fairytale, or once upon a time
look at the truth, and see what you have done
you've risked everything, are you sure they will be there for you?

I've stayed true to my core beliefs
I have been firm, and have been always fair
and I am so disappointed, the way you've behaved
and for what? you've acted like a stupid fool.

So to be again your father's daughter
you must look again, at your whole life's history
look back in life, who had been there for you?
and have the humility and good grace to say you know I am right.

TO SARAH - A RAY OF HOPE

(A prayer for the brave)

As the darkness falls down all around you
and your burden seem to grow and grow
in despair you seek salvation
just a ray of hope, to light your way.

Adversity will find you courage
although it seems all hope is doomed
just remember what I first told you
that your strength will come, from within your truth.

Salvation yes, it may be hiding
in plain sight, though you cannot see
cast your mind back to your darkest moments
and remember how you made it through.

This time around, you've coped much quicker
where you've stayed true to your core beliefs
though everyone is trying to hurt you
you're doing well, just keep fighting.

Yet the very milk of human kindness
like a beacon, it shines through you.
if you believe there is a karma
you will get yours, and they'll get theirs.

So don't despair, and your faith you'll keep
all the sh*t you've faced will make you stronger
just believe there's a guardian angel
and better still, you will find your peace.

TO MORGAN - A CHILD'S EYE VIEW?

(A life without responsibilities)

In the cold dark winter's mornings
when all I want to do is sleep
when mum says 'now it's time to wake'
because school time, it just will not wait.

I cry and moan, and feel so bad
and want to stay in bed
and sleep until I want to wake
then play at home with my toys instead.

But no, I rise, and get ready too
packed lunch, and books to school
what do you know, when I get there
the fun day just begins.

A normal life is pretty drab, and sometimes seem so hard
and it's normal too, to have a dream

a fantasy life, a life so free
a life without responsibility.

It's all your fault, why can't I sleep?
I only go to school for you
why don't you ever think of me?
I know what is best for me.

Get over it, there is no such thing
so a humdrum life it is
you go to school because it's good for you
and it's the best thing you will ever do.

TO ELIZE (14 YEARS)
– the path of self-destruction

If someone takes away your freedom
then turns the lights off in your sky
and you find yourself out in the cold and darkness
you'll wonder why it went so far.

The choice you are making is self-destruction
you're about to learn the harshest truth
there is no such thing as cost-free living
without the love and support of those who care.

you may think you're being clever
or you feel so strong and full of fight
but who are you hurting most of all?
it is your life, you are destroying.

Think it through, you stupid child
who is there to keep you warm?
who takes care of all your wishes?
who nurtured you throughout your life?

You have chosen the path of self-destruction
despite your truth, you can clearly see
you want to blame the world around you
and punish everyone but you.

It's not too late to see the wisdom
and put your life on the right track
but if you choose the path of darkness
there's no one there but yourself to blame.

THE CHRYSALIS
- Emerging From The Darkest Place

From a long way back, in the darkest place
there has always been a ray of light
sometimes you just could not see
there would be strength from your adversity.

It really has been the longest time
since you felt the sunshine on your face
now you're getting stronger, all the time
now your adversaries are not the same.

From their harshest words, from their vicious tongues
to keep you on your knees, they played along
now when the nasty words are spoken
just send them back, with a cricket bat.

The light ahead you can clearly see
now the scales of doubts have been broken
never, ever, doubt yourself
or they will send you back, into the dark.

Self-belief and self-preservation
are the turning point to guide your life
you don't need this fool to tell you
you've sacrificed your love for him.

So stand up tall, you have been tested
you've found the answers within yourself
don't be afraid, you've faced their worst
what can they do, except to curse?

Now looking back, you can clearly see
to self-sacrifice and to give selflessly
has only encouraged the secret bullies
to take from you, and never give.

So there is a lesson to be learnt
Self-respect, and putting one's self first
is the first requisite for a happy life
then you can give what they deserve.

WALKING A MILE IN YOUR FATHER'S SHOES

(why there is no apology)

For all the hate that you can muster
for the animosity and anger that you feel
for the sense of betrayal that overwhelms you
you've lashed out with a venomous shrill.

You feel your dad has turned against you,
for others, not worthy of my love
you even went as far as saying
I bullied you, to get my way.

Now think back to when you were eleven
when the hate and the anger were mine to bear
my sense of betrayal was even greater
than you can imagine yours to be.

So why have we faced this test of character?
and how did we deal with it, in our own way?
what were the reasons for my anger?
and what is it, for yours today?

You say your sister has come between us
because I stand right by her side
and destroyed the wedding day of your other sister
then carelessly, I just walked away.

My anger was for the way I was treated,
which I had seen with my own two eyes
the way I felt then has never altered
yet the way I have behaved has never changed.

You've lashed out at every opportunity
yet you cannot say one thing she has done
to hurt you, direct or indirectly
because the simple truth is, she never has.

So five minutes in your father's shoes
and you cannot hide the hurt you feel
and you still cannot recognize that,
after sixteen years, I've never verbalized anyone.

I stood firm, for all my true principles
and have always been true, to myself
if this gets in the way of your own affection,
then I rest my case, and so be it.

TO SARAH - CHRISTMAS 2012

(a Christmas wish that must come true.)

Christmas is the time of year
when we reflect on the year gone by
it's a time of peace and happiness
when we should all be feeling glad.

Yet this year, like the two before
has brought you a lot of hurt and tears
and what I wish for you the most
is the kind of peace that you deserve.

If you can only find your peace
the kind that's found within
you'll see that there's a better way
to live your life at ease.

Your peace is there, it's in plain sight
although you can't believe
it starts by looking at yourself
and looking from within.

At first you must be comfortable
with everything you are and do
be sure the mirror you do not fear
because your heart is true and fair.

Then after that you can be at ease
and show your foes no fear
give to them as they give to you
without a second thought.

if you can find the sense of calm
that comes with peace within
then all the troubles you have faced
will fall in line and take their place.

To be at peace with yourself
and to have that self-belief
it's really what it's all about.
Your self-respect, you must put first
and damn the ones that don't deserve.

So there is a lesson to be learnt
Self-respect, and putting one's self first
is the first requisite, for a happy life
then you can give, what they deserve.

THE LAST SUPPER? (LUNCH TODAY)

(The Teacher's Tale)

What lessons can we learn today?
we, the teachers from our holy school
are we the guardians of our futures bright?
or just the squabbles of our selfish ways?

We, the teachers of our nation's young
we preach to them, what they are expected of
to learn about our giving, and our humanities
and how we should be willing to give for free.

We sat and had the breaking of bread
and share our joys, with some sadness
yet when the bill for our feast arrived
something changed - now it's one for one.

It was so embarrassing
the petty fights, for a few pennies
what can our children learn from this?
have they had it right, all along?

They are happy to share someone else's toys
and take from them, what is not their own
but when it comes to sharing theirs
now that's a different story
(my teachers said so all night long).

A GRIEF TODAY

A Tribute To Pat Creamer/Glenon RIP December 2013

I am on my knees in tears and in pain
As I try to absorb this sad news today
A real true friend who I worshipped and revered
Had passed away before I could see her.

I've known her since I was thirteen
I really thought the world of her.
She had the biggest heart anyone could know
She'd had hard times that no one deserved.

If I gather up all of my troubled times
And then multiply by ten, and then add some more
It would still pale into insignificance
To the burdens you carried, with your ill health and strife.

So Pat I'm really sorry now
To know you're gone, but never forgotten
There's a special place, in my heart I will keep
For the giants of life that has touched my life.

We cannot turn back the hand of time
Though I really feel I have let you down
I should have done more to help and support you
When you were alive, when it really mattered.

Words by Harry Harefield. (James - your bodyguard)

AS WE SAID OUR LAST GOODBYE

(The Funeral of Pat Creamer/Glenon)

It felt more like an autumn morning
As we came to say our last farewell
There were beautiful words in church were spoken
When we came outside, for you – the sun was shining.

It was the happy day that you had requested,
So many were there, all of us with the same voices
The beauty of your heart, it was well recounted
As the wonderful words for you they were spoken.

So Pat you really shone a light
And touched everyone who'd ever met you
I feel so proud that my words were recorded
For you've given hope to the whole human race.

Words by Harry Harefield. (James - your bodyguard)

BV - #0270 - 230326 - C0 - 203/127/17 - PB - 9781861511331 - Matt Lamination